RUFUS NORRIS

As a director recent theatre includes *Peribanez* and *Afore Night Come* for the Young Vic, *Small Change* for Sheffield Crucible, *Dirty Butterfly* for Soho Theatre, *Under the Blue Sky* for the Royal Court and *Mish Alla Ruman*, a comedy in Arabic about the Intifada for Al Kasaba Theatre in Ramallah, Palestine.

Music-theatre work includes *Tall Stories* (BAC, Vienna Festival) and *Sea Tongue* with The Shout, as well as *Pierrot* by Orlando Gough.

He has directed a number of other plays at the Royal Court, Birmingham Rep, Pleasance London and the Gate Theatre.

He is co-artistic director of Wink, for whom he has directed *Strike Gently Away from Body*, *The People Downstairs* and *the art of random whistling* (Young Vic Studio), *Rosa Carnivora*, *Waking Beauty* and *The Lizzie Play* (Arts Threshold, national tours, Hong Kong).

As well as *Sleeping Beauty*, he wrote the libretto for *On Thee We Feed* for ENO Baylis and co-wrote *Strike Gently Away from Body* for Wink.

He was given the Evening Standard Outstanding Newcomer Award in 2001 for *Afore Night Come*, and was awarded an Arts Foundation Fellowship in 2002. He is Associate Director at the Young Vic.

Other Adaptations in this Series

ANIMAL FARM
Ian Wooldridge
Adapted from George Orwell

ANNA KARENINA
Helen Edmundson
Adapted from Leo Tolstoy

ARTHUR & GEORGE
David Edgar
Adapted from Julian Barnes

BEAUTY AND THE BEAST
Laurence Boswell

THE CANTERBURY TALES
Mike Poulton
Adapted from Geoffrey Chaucer

A CHRISTMAS CAROL
Karen Louise Hebden
Adapted from Charles Dickens

CINDERELLA
Stuart Paterson

CORAM BOY
Helen Edmundson
Adapted from Jamila Gavin

DAVID COPPERFIELD
Alastair Cording
Adapted from Charles Dickens

DR JEKYLL AND MR HYDE
David Edgar
Adapted from Robert Louis Stevenson

DRACULA
Liz Lochhead
Adapted from Bram Stoker

EMMA
Martin Millar and Doon MacKichan
Adapted from Jane Austen

FAR FROM THE MADDING CROWD
Mark Healy
Adapted from Thomas Hardy

GREAT EXPECTATIONS
Nick Ormerod and Declan Donnellan
Adapted from Charles Dickens

HANSEL AND GRETEL
Stuart Paterson

HIS DARK MATERIALS
Nicholas Wright
Adapted from Philip Pullman

JANE EYRE
Polly Teale
Adapted from Charlotte Brontë

THE JUNGLE BOOK
Stuart Paterson
Adapted from Rudyard Kipling

KENSUKE'S KINGDOM
Stuart Paterson
Adapted from Michael Morpurgo

KES
Lawrence Till
Adapted from Barry Hines

MADAME BOVARY
Fay Weldon
Adapted from Gustave Flaubert

MARY BARTON
Rona Munro
Adapted from Elizabeth Gaskell

THE MILL ON THE FLOSS
Helen Edmundson
Adapted from George Eliot

NORTHANGER ABBEY
Tim Luscombe
Adapted from Jane Austen

NOUGHTS & CROSSES
Dominic Cooke
Adapted from Malorie Blackman

PERSUASION
Mark Healy
Adapted from Jane Austen

THE RAILWAY CHILDREN
Mike Kenny
Adapted from E. Nesbit

SENSE AND SENSIBILITY
Mark Healy
Adapted from Jane Austen

SUNSET SONG
Alastair Cording
Adapted from Lewis Grassic Gibbon

TREASURE ISLAND
Stuart Paterson
Adapted from Robert Louis Stevenson

WAR AND PEACE
Helen Edmundson
Adapted from Leo Tolstoy

Rufus Norris

SLEEPING BEAUTY

from
The Sleeping Beauty in the Woods
by Charles Perrault

NICK HERN BOOKS
London
www.nickhernbooks.co.uk

A Nick Hern Book

Sleeping Beauty first published in Great Britain in 2003 as a paperback original by Nick Hern Books Limited, 14 Larden Road, London W3 7ST

Reprinted 2008, 2010, 2011, 2012

Typeset by Country Setting, Kingsdown, Kent CT14 8ES
Printed and bound in Great Britain by Mimeo Ltd, Cambridgeshire PE29 6XX

A CIP catalogue record for this book is available from the British Library

ISBN 978 1 85459 742 7

Woodland
CARBON
www.woodlandcarbon.co.uk
NICK HERN BOOKS
Printed on Carbon Captured paper

FOR LOUIS
AND HIS GRANDAD

CASTING NOTES

The original production of this play had a cast of four women and six men, with most actors playing more than one character. However, the cast size could be expanded considerably, in the following ways:

Goody Though written for one actor, this part could easily be divided into two or three parts:

Goody One is the Goody we meet at the beginning of the play. She meets the Prince of Questions and tells him the story of what happens; she meets the Ogress, and travels to the Castle, where she prevents her from eating the baby Prince.

Goody Two is the younger Goody that we see in flashback. She meets King and Queen Beauty in the forest, goes to the Palace, issues the curse and spins the dress for Beauty's birthday. Her last appearance is when she creates the thorn forest and witnesses the disappearance of King and Queen Beauty.

Goody Three is the oldest Goody, who we first meet when the Prince surprises her in the forest. She takes him to the thorns and the Sleeping Beauty, and she is there throughout the second half.

The three parts are of roughly equal size.

Fairies In this version the fairies that bless the baby Beauty were not actors but made of cloth and sticks, and Goody is greatly offended by this. It would be possible to change this so that they could be played by several performers, who might dance and sing the blessing song to the baby. Two lines on page 24 would have to change, as follows:

QUEEN. Stop it! We've had our own beautiful fairy costumes made, we certainly don't need a real fairy. She's filthy, filthy, filthy! Etc . . .

And on page 26:

GOODY. Fairies? Call you these fairies? Humans in pretty
clothes! Are you so afraid of nature, etc . . .

Hector and Rose In the original production the children were
dolls which made no sound. These parts could be played by
two young performers, in which case some fun could be had
with finding points when they might cry or respond to what is
going on.

Slaves, Courtiers, Forest Creatures The number of
performers required for these roles is obviously very flexible.
There should be at least four Courtiers (not including the
Minstrel) and enough Slaves to bring on the table and chairs at
the beginning of the second half, though for both there could
be many more.

STAGING NOTES

In the original production the play was performed 'in the round'. However, it was written to be performed in any configuration and could be presented as successfully in a traditional proscenium (or 'end-on') manner, a thrust stage with audience on three sides, or even in promenade, or 'walkabout'.

The first production had a series of trapdoors in the stage floor, as well as several other entrances. Though very useful, traps are by no means essential and the play could easily be staged without any, as long as there are several entrances onto the performing area. The intention was that any director, producer or designer should be as bold as they like about staging it, but should it be useful there are a few scenes or potential challenges worth mentioning.

The play takes place in three locations, each requiring a different energy and atmosphere.

The Forest The forest is a place of energy and life. Nature is not clean and ordered, and it is important to establish that. It should feel unkempt and slightly chaotic – not overtly dangerous but frightening to an outsider. This can be achieved as much through sound as anything. It requires places where Forest Creatures might hide generally, and specifically a place where Goody can hide (her groundhole, or den) and lock the Ogre (preferably that he can escape from without being seen, as it would be a long time to wait if he was stuck in there).

The Palace The Palace is the opposite of the Forest, a place of order and cleanliness keeping filthy nature at bay.

The principal staging challenge within the Palace is the bed on which Beauty sleeps, as she is on it for a fair amount of time. This might be at some place on, below or above the stage. Alternatively it could be carried off by the Courtiers after she has been placed on it, and brought back on by them sleepwalking just before the kiss.

The spindle used in the original production was not a full spinning wheel, and this could have been simplified even further. The important event is the pricking on the needle, and the appearance and disappearance of the spindle need not involve any great pyrotechnics.

The Castle This is the dark place, where chaos masquerades as order, and fear is the ruler.

In all three environments, the differences between them were emphasised almost entirely through atmosphere – there was almost no 'scenery' as such. This allowed a very swift and fluid movement from one to the next without pausing. The use of sound and light were pivotal, and often in a surprisingly simple way.

There are various other challenges – the appearances of the thorns, the cloth for the new dress, etc. These and others are related to Goody's spells – the magic – and a bold approach to this will provide ample cover for the necessary developments, however they are to be achieved.

Acknowledgement

Waking Beauty, written by Deirdre Strath, based on the Perrault fairytale, was produced at Arts Threshold in 1994. Several members of the *Sleeping Beauty* company, including the director and designer, were involved in that production which was the original inspiration for this show.

Sleeping Beauty in this version was first performed at the Young Vic Theatre, London, on 22 November 2002. Press night was 4 December 2002. The cast was as follows:

GOODY	Helena Lymbery
THE OGRE	Christopher Brand
PRINCE OF QUESTIONS	Paul Ewing
QUEEN	Katie Quentin
KING	Miltos Yerolemou
THE MINSTREL	Hazel Holder
BEAUTY	Danielle King
THE OGRESS	Daniel Cerqueira
THE TABLESLAVE	Duncan Wisbey
THE PRINCE	James Loye

Directed by   Rufus Norris

Designed by   Katrina Lindsay

Lighting by   Tim Mitchell

Music composed by   Richard Chew

Sound by   Paul Arditti

SLEEPING BEAUTY

CHARACTERS

The Forest

GOODY, *a scruffy old fairy, and flatulent*

PRINCE OF QUESTIONS, *a lost prince*

OGRE, *huge and terrifying*

FOREST CREATURES, *strange but harmless*

THORNS, *who protect the Sleeping Beauty, and are not nice*

The Palace

KING BEAUTY, *well-meaning but weak*

QUEEN BEAUTY, *highly strung and squeaky clean*

BEAUTY, *their daughter; beautiful but spirited*

MINSTREL, *who only sings, and has a bad attitude*

COURTIERS

The Castle

OGRESS, *a Queen with something to hide*

PRINCE, *her son, dashing and brave*

TABLE-SLAVE, *a slave with his head permanently through a table*

DONKEY *and* GOAT, *pets of the Table-Slave*

SLAVES

ACT ONE

In the forest. At the centre of stage a spindle, which slowly turns.

FOREST CREATURE (*sung*).
Once upon a time
Once upon a place in a different time . . .

Dawn breaks, the spindle disappears and the forest slowly comes to life, with strange creatures appearing from everywhere.

seed and acorn hoof and horn
all that dies must be reborn
from dusk til dawn til eve til morn
flesh shall grow then grow forlorn.

GOODY, *a very shabby fairy, appears from her den.*

GOODY. Oh no . . . another day.

FOREST CREATURE (*sung*).
love and anger joy and scorn
soon must fade, so soon must fade
for all shall meet with death's sharp thorn
then flower anew come sun and dawn
seed and acorn hoof and horn
all that dies must be reborn
from dusk til dawn til eve til morn
flesh shall grow then grow forlorn.

OGRE (*off*). Humaan!

The sound of flight everywhere and FOREST CREATURES *disappear, leaving* GOODY *alone, who goes back into her den. A terrified man runs on. He is the* PRINCE OF QUESTIONS. *He sprints straight across the stage.*

(*Off.*) Humaan!

He sprints back on, climbs into GOODY*'s den and is chased out.*

GOODY. Ow ow ow.

PRINCE OF QUESTIONS. Aaaaahaaaar.

GOODY. What's the matter with you?

PRINCE OF QUESTIONS. I'm frightened!

GOODY. You are, aren't you.

PRINCE OF QUESTIONS. Aren't you frightened?

GOODY. Of what?

PRINCE OF QUESTIONS. The Ogre!

GOODY. Oh the Ogre. No.

PRINCE OF QUESTIONS. Why not?

GOODY. I's a fairy.

PRINCE OF QUESTIONS. So?

GOODY. We taste very bitter. So no Ogre eats us.

PRINCE OF QUESTIONS. Oh.

GOODY. They just eat humans.

PRINCE OF QUESTIONS. Aah.

GOODY. It's alright. Part of Ogre nature, eating humans.

PRINCE OF QUESTIONS. Aah.

GOODY. Part of human nature, running away.

OGRE (*off*). Humaan.

PRINCE OF QUESTIONS. Aaah! What's fairy nature?

GOODY. To do good.

PRINCE OF QUESTIONS. Well can't you do some good and help me, I'm just a poor prince and I've never hurt anyone and . . .

GOODY. A prince? You're a prince?

PRINCE OF QUESTIONS. Yes.

OGRE (*off*). Humaan!

> GOODY *hides the* PRINCE OF QUESTIONS *behind her. A huge ogre appears – large, hairy, and generally terrifying. The* OGRE *and* GOODY *scowl at each other.*
>
> Fairee.

GOODY. Yes. So away and leave me be.

OGRE. Where's the humaan?

GOODY. That way, you great pudden.

He starts to go but stops, sniffs the air and turns back to GOODY.

What? Don't you come near and stink maggoty breathing on me, or I'll set fire to your hairy backside.

OGRE. I can smell him. Where's my humaan?

GOODY *shuffles round, trying to keep away.*

GOODY. Calm you now, no humans here, oh cramps Goody thinks, thinks fast now . . .

OGRE. He's mine, give him to me.

The OGRE *forces* GOODY *over, revealing the* PRINCE OF QUESTIONS.

PRINCE OF QUESTIONS. Aaaahaaaar.

OGRE. HUMAAN.

The OGRE *grabs him and drags him away, but* GOODY *distracts him. He stops and chases her, and she stuffs his mouth with herbs. She hangs on for dear life as he tries to get the herbs out, slowing until he drops, asleep.*

PRINCE OF QUESTIONS. What's happened?

GOODY. He's eaten half my remedies, the great fatgut! He'll be asleep a while I expect. Ogres are so stupid. But you're a Prince?

PRINCE OF QUESTIONS. Yes, but what if he wakes up?

GOODY. He won't.

PRINCE OF QUESTIONS. But if you're a fairy, why didn't you do a proper spell back then?

GOODY. Fairy business.

PRINCE OF QUESTIONS. But why couldn't you?

GOODY. Eek! I didn't do a spell because I couldn't. Because I have no spells left. Anyway.

PRINCE OF QUESTIONS. But why not?

GOODY. Because.

PRINCE OF QUESTIONS. Because what?

GOODY. Because! Because I did a bad thing, and I lost my fairy power. If I undo the bad thing by making it good again, I might get it back. And now I can, if you really are a . . .

PRINCE OF QUESTIONS. But what about him? What if he wakes?

GOODY. Alright, alright.

She starts to bundle the OGRE *into her den.*

PRINCE OF QUESTIONS. Where are you taking him?

GOODY. Just into my groundhole til he comes round.

PRINCE OF QUESTIONS. But can't you tie him up? Give him more remedies? Kill him?

GOODY. No.

PRINCE OF QUESTIONS. Why not?

GOODY. I's a fairy.

PRINCE OF QUESTIONS. So?

GOODY. Fairies meant to do good. Anyway, if a fairy kills, the fairy dies.

She locks the OGRE *in her den.*

Now. Be you a proper prince?

PRINCE OF QUESTIONS. Father's a king, Mother's a queen, is that enough?

GOODY. A prince! At last, a prince! And I nearly let you get eaten! Be rich, prince?

PRINCE OF QUESTIONS. No, but why?

GOODY. Be married, prince?

PRINCE OF QUESTIONS. No, but why?

GOODY. Be brave, prince?

PRINCE OF QUESTIONS. No er yes, But why?

GOODY. Because up there, just up there's a palace, and in that palace be a sleeping princess, the most beautiful princess as ever breathed.

PRINCE OF QUESTIONS. Where? Why can't I see her?

GOODY. She's there, trust I, and only a Prince can wake her. All you needs do is kiss her and she's yours for ever, with palace, wealth and all.

PRINCE OF QUESTIONS. But if it's that easy, why hasn't anyone else kissed her? What if I don't like her? What if she doesn't like me? And how do you know this? How did she get there? Why is she asleep? Who put her to sleep? Why won't you tell me?

GOODY. I'll tell you!

PRINCE OF QUESTIONS. But . . .

GOODY. Be quiet, and just listen, and I'll tell you. Once upon a time a few years back and very close to here, a young fairy I was with no troubles on me and a happy existence, all my spells were working, doing good and such, when into my life one night there come two visitors to this forest. Here see.

She throws a powder (story dust) from her pocket into the air. Suddenly it is night in a very spooky and alive forest. KING screams from off.

QUEEN. Fairy Goody? Fairy Goody?

They come on together, clutching each other and petrified.

KING. My dear wife, turn back I beg you!

QUEEN. Onward husband, we must. Fairy Goody.

KING. Where are our guards?

QUEEN. They are driven away, the cowards, all run off . . . Fairy Goody?

A forest creature crosses their path.

KING. Oh! My heart, my heart is failing.

QUEEN. Get up! Steel yourself, my true heart, and be brave.

More creatures appear.

Ugh! Husband!

KING. Wife! Ugh! Wife!

QUEEN. Husband!

KING *and* QUEEN. Ugh!

QUEEN. Get back, get back you heathen beasts.

KING. I beg you, wife, go back with me.

A forest creature charges across between them, and then off.

Why did we come here? Why are we not home? Where is she?

QUEEN. Where are you? Fairy Goody force of goodness and life? Fairy Goody?

The forest quietens immediately as GOODY *appears. They step back.*

GOODY. Evening.

QUEEN screams.

KING. Get back, get back! What do you want from us?

GOODY. I want nothing. Tis you were calling I.

KING. What?

GOODY. I's fairy Goody. You did call, just.

KING. You?

QUEEN. You can't be a fairy, you're all . . . she's not what we wanted at all, husband.

GOODY. I's gone, then.

Forest goes loopy again. KING *and* QUEEN *scream.*

KING. No, no, fairy please!

Forest calms again.

Please, we're thankful to you for appearing, forgive our lack of civility . . . we're a little unnerved, you see.

GOODY. Yes you are. What is it you want?

KING. Well ... um ... the queen and I have, for many years ...

QUEEN. A child. We want a child.

GOODY. Yes you do.

QUEEN. Pardon?

GOODY. Humans want children, that's what they do. Very well.

KING. What?

QUEEN. Pardon?

GOODY. Very well. Your desire is great, to bring you here, and love will follow. I will give you your child.

QUEEN. Oh yes, oh yes.

KING. Do you hear, my life, she can do it, and she will! Our loneliness is ended!

QUEEN. But how will you deliver it to the palace? Should we send someone? What are you doing?

GOODY *casts a spell, and everything goes strange.*

GOODY. Mother Green of harsh and mild
Blindfell meek and turnbeech wild
All good bound and reconciled
Fill this belly now with child.

The QUEEN *becomes heavily pregnant on the spot.*

QUEEN. Oh, oh.

KING. How wonderful . . .

QUEEN. How shocking.

GOODY *farts loudly, and the* QUEEN *faints.*

KING. Was that really necessary?

GOODY. Comes with the magic. So, tis done. You have a month to prepare, and take rest.

KING. The baby . . . I can feel it moving.

GOODY. She, to be particular.

KING. She?

GOODY. It is a girl. I only do girls.

KING. A daughter! Wake up, wife, it's a daughter, our own sweet little beauty!

QUEEN. What? What? Oh. . I thought I would get a baby.

GOODY. Life without birth is unnatural, and I cannot do that. This last joyful task of birthing is your own.

QUEEN. I'd rather hoped to avoid that bit.

KING. I will cover you with gold for this, Fairy, no more hedge-dwelling for you.

GOODY. I want for no gold, King. I am a fairy, and do good for its own rewards.

QUEEN. I'm feeling dreadfully uncomfortable and what's that terrible smell?

KING. She did a . . . um . . .

QUEEN. Husband, can we leave this place?

KING. Of course. Thank you, Goody.

QUEEN. Husband, please let's go . . . (*Exits.*)

KING. The palace will glow with the wonder of what you have given us –

GOODY. I'm glad.

KING. – and her naming-day will be the most joyous ever witnessed in our kingdom.

GOODY. Really?

KING. Oh yes, there'll be fireworks, and feasting, and a whole throng of fairies to give her the blessing of an angel.

GOODY. Can I come?

QUEEN (*off*). Husband!

KING. Umm.

GOODY. I never have been to a naming-day, nor to a palace neither.

QUEEN (*off*). Husband.

GOODY. I would love to come.

KING. And so you shall; it is the very least. And, Fairy Goody, you shall be our guest, our guest of the highest honour!

QUEEN (*off*). Husband!

GOODY *throws story dust, and the scene returns as before.*

PRINCE OF QUESTIONS. How did you do that? Didn't you say your spells had run out?

GOODY. Story dust. It's not a spell, just herbs. Thyme, mostly. So listen.

PRINCE OF QUESTIONS. And how did you do that incredible fart?

GOODY. It is a side-effect, from the force of the magic. Humans are so squeamish. Now will you listen?

PRINCE OF QUESTIONS. What to?

GOODY. So that was the start of the whole, and would have been just fine if people had kept to what they'd promised, but people never do.

PRINCE OF QUESTIONS. Why? What happened?

GOODY. Nothing, that's what. When the time came for the birthing of the babe I heard nothing. They hadn't invited me. So I went to the palace to see for myself. (*Throws story dust, and hides, watching.*)

The Palace.

The courtiers and minstrel are decorating the space, running into position at the entrance of the QUEEN. *They support the* QUEEN*'s cause where appropriate.*

QUEEN. No!

KING. But I promised.

QUEEN. No.

KING. My sweet.

QUEEN. Utterly no.

KING. But I gave my word we'd invite her, and she is the cause of our joy, my lovely.

QUEEN. No, no, no, no, no!

KING. But wife . . .

QUEEN. She actually passed wind in front of me!

KING. That was because of the power of the spell.

QUEEN. Stop it! We've had our own beautiful fairies made. We certainly don't need a real one. She's filthy, filthy, filthy! I'm feeling faint at the thought of it.

KING. My only heart, I gave my word and I am the King.

QUEEN. Oh! And a fine King you are, whose word is worth more than the well-being of your wife and child! Heartless, proud man!

KING. Oh don't be like that, squidgy.

The COURTIERS *snigger. The* QUEEN *wails at him, and the courtiers join in.*

Very well, very well! We shan't invite her.

QUEEN. Good! Thank you!

She goes. The courtiers applaud.

KING. Have you quite finished.

The courtiers leave, except the minstrel.

Oh no . . .

MINSTREL (*sung*).
    Oh no, oh no.

KING. And you can stop that, you leathered old squark-bucket. I know. I promised the fairy, but what can I do?

MINSTREL (*sung*).
    What can you do, what can you do . . .

KING. Shut up. Maybe I could get a message to her, an apology.

MINSTREL (*sung*).
    . . . with all your broken promises.

KING. Silence!

The MINSTREL *tuts and leaves.*

Blasted fairy . . .

GOODY *appears.*

What? How did you . . .

GOODY. You promised me.

KING. I know, I know, look I know, but . . .

GOODY. You said I was to be guest of honour.

The blessing song begins as the QUEEN, MINSTREL *and courtiers approach.*

KING. Oh no! Look you're here now, and welcome, if you can keep out of sight. Only there's an awful row to be had if you're seen . . . Now be silent, and watch from here.

COURTIERS (*sung*).
Blessings, blessings
Rain down on sweet beauty
Blessings, blessings
Blessings upon you.

The baby BEAUTY *is brought in on a cushion, with* COURTIERS *carrying fake fairies, followed by the* QUEEN. *The* KING *tries to make sure* GOODY *isn't seen.*

QUEEN. The Royal Princess Beauty!

GOODY. What are those?

KING. They're our very own fairies, we had them made specially.

QUEEN. Beautiful as morning
Graceful as the sunrise
The voice of an angel
And the blue sky in your open eyes.

Despite the KING's *efforts,* GOODY *comes forward to look at her.*

KING. No!

GOODY. I just want to see her.

QUEEN. What is she doing here? Oh help me, husband, Guards!

KING. She just appeared, my love, I didn't . . .

QUEEN. Out, out! Guards!

The COURTIERS *advance, but* GOODY *knocks them down with a throw of magic.*

Oh my poor weak heart! Husband, rid me of this repungance.

GOODY. I gave her you, that babe.

QUEEN. Don't you dare touch her! Go back to your place of darkness and chaos! Within these walls there must only be light – my clean, beautiful fairies have given her all she needs, how could you bless her more, except with your dirt and filthy disease!

GOODY. Fairies? Call you these fairies? Cloth on sticks! Are you so afraid of nature you make pretend? For all your light and shiny floors you couldn't make that child, you needed nature, you needed me. But you broke your promise. You do not deserve her. So now I will bless her. Bless her with a life without you.

She spells.

Henbane and Monkshed, Nightshade and worse
Gather you here, and honour my curse:
She'll be pricked so by a spindle
And sleep the months away
A hundred years or more she'll lie
Until there comes a day
When with a kiss she woken is
But only by a prince
Her sleeping eyes are all you'll see
And all your tears shall rinse.

GOODY *farts loudly. They all faint or run from the smell, except the* KING. *He takes the baby, looks at* GOODY, *and exits.*

KING (*sung*).
Beautiful as morning
Graceful as the sunrise
The voice of an angel
And the blue sky in your open eyes.

GOODY *flicks a little story dust, and the first scene returns.*

PRINCE OF QUESTIONS. What. . ? Why . . . ?

GOODY. That was when everything went bad. My spells started going wrong, and my Goody wings all but fell off. If you lose your wings, fairy life is ended then, and I don't know what horrors happen. And I was so sorry, so full of remorse and nothing to be done to make right again.

PRINCE OF QUESTIONS. But is there a baby up there? Can I marry a baby?

GOODY. Listen then. So the curse of the spindle was given, but none knew when it would come round.

PRINCE OF QUESTIONS. What's a spindle?

GOODY. Tis the spike on the spinning wheel, the maker of thread and source of all cloth. You never saw one?

PRINCE OF QUESTIONS. A poor person's thing, is it?

GOODY. It is. Poor King, he banned all use of them throughout the land, so there were no new clothes for fifteen years, and he never let Beauty outside the palace walls, however she tried . . .

She throws story dust, and the QUEEN *and courtiers come to life.*

MINSTREL. Beauty?

TUTTI. Beauty? Beauty, where are you? (*etc.*)

QUEEN. Where is she, where is she?

COURTIER 1. She's not in the gardens, highness.

COURTIER 2. Nor the stables.

COURTIER 3. She's not in the dungeon.

COURTIER 4. Or the midden heap.

COURTIER 5. Or the moat.

MINSTREL (*sung*).
    She's gone! She's gone, she's gone.

QUEEN. How many times has this happened this week? You incontinent fools!

COURTIERS. It was him ma'am (*etc*) . . .

QUEEN. Silence! She must be somewhere, she can't have disappeared . . .

COURTIERS. I think she probably has (*etc*) . . .

QUEEN. Beauty, Beauty where are you? Has she gone? Has she finally been taken from us, and the day before her birthday . . .

COURTIERS. Sadly, the chances of disappearing on such a day are (*etc*) . . .

QUEEN. Oh beauty!

She exits, leaving the courtiers arguing. They stop suddenly and hide, as BEAUTY *appears from somewhere unexpected.*

PRINCE OF QUESTIONS. She's beautiful . . .

GOODY. Shh . . .

BEAUTY *looks around to make sure she is alone, then tries to escape from the palace. She is prevented by the courtiers.*

COURTIERS. No, no, no (*etc*) . . .

BEAUTY. Oh No! Leave me alone! I was just going to have a look! Right.

She runs to the other side, is prevented again, and so on until the courtiers are holding on to her as she struggles to escape.

COURTIERS. No, no, no.

BEAUTY. Let me go, let me go!

QUEEN. Put her down!

The QUEEN *claps her hands and the courtiers put her down.*

KING. You really must stop doing that, my dear! How many times must we tell you that you're safest indoors?

BEAUTY. But Father.

QUEEN. It's not funny, and it's not mature.

BEAUTY. But it's so boring being locked up in this dreary palace all day, every day. Why can't I go out, just once?

The forest looks just so dark, so twisty and alive, and I am
nearly sixteen you know.

KING. Not until tomorrow, my love, and even then.

QUEEN. Listen to me young lady. There's many things you
don't know about, and many you don't want to know about.

BEAUTY. I do, I do . . .

QUEEN. You've everything you want here, everything you
need.

BEAUTY. Boring, boring, boring.

QUEEN. That's enough of that.

BEAUTY. But.

QUEEN. No, utterly no. It's a word you seem to have trouble
understanding, so you need us to guide you –

BEAUTY. – and give me lectures.

KING. Rules are not lectures. A world without order is a world
of fear, where –

BEAUTY. – where joy is a stranger and danger is near, I know,
I know.

QUEEN. Enough! It's time for bed. Ablutions!

The COURTIERS *and* MINSTREL *exit.*

BEAUTY. Oh no . . .

QUEEN. Daughter.

BEAUTY. I'm perfectly capable of brushing my own teeth.

KING. But we don't want you catching any nasty germs.

BEAUTY. Why does everything have to be so safe? Why can't
anything exciting happen?

QUEEN. Oh Beauty. You must take control of these feelings of
frustration, and just say no. Just say no.

COURTIERS *and* MINSTREL *sing Just Say No, while they
prepare her for sleep.*

QUEEN (*sung*).
If you're ever faced with the forces of temptation.

TUTTI. Just say No, just say No.

KING. And if you meet a person of uncertain reputation
Just say No, just say No.

COURTIER 1. If he tries to offer you some dubious vegetation
Just say No, just say No.

COURTIER 2. If he plays you music with a good vibration
Just say No, just say No.

COURTIER 3. If you feel like singing a demonic incantation
Just say No, just say No.

COURTIER 4. If you think it might be fun to try decapitation
Just say No, just say No.

MINSTREL. And if you find a bottle of your mother's
medication.

QUEEN. I beg your pardon?

TUTTI. Just say No, just say No
Now you know the only way to curb imagination
Just say No, just say no . . .

QUEEN. Now do you understand?

BEAUTY. No.

KING. What?

BEAUTY. Of course I do! I know you're just being careful,
and I love you for it, but it is my birthday tomorrow and I
don't feel very spoilt right now.

KING. You shall be spoilt to the high heavens in the morning,
my dearest.

QUEEN. So you just make sure you get to bed early, and sleep
well. We don't want you tired and grumpy on your birthday,
do we?

BEAUTY. I'm sixteen tomorrow, not six.

QUEEN. Enough! Now I think everyone's got work to do.
Goodnight Darling.

BEAUTY. Good night mother.

QUEEN *and courtiers exit, except minstrel.*

Father.

KING. Yes.

BEAUTY. There is one special gift I'd like to ask for.

KING. You can't go outside, we've told you.

BEAUTY. I know! It's not that.

KING. Then what, my precious?

BEAUTY. A new dress.

KING. A new . . . oh.

BEAUTY. All my dresses are old, most of them were mother's, and the others are made out of old curtains.

KING. Those were very fine curtains, from the mountains of –

BEAUTY. I'm a princess! And I want a new dress, just one.

KING. It's just not that simple, my dear.

BEAUTY. I thought you loved me.

Silence.

KING. Well you'll have to wait and see. Surprises wouldn't be surprising if –

BEAUTY. – one wasn't surprised, I know, and that means I won't get one.

KING. You will! Or at least you might, um.

BEAUTY. You said I will!

KING. No, I said.

BEAUTY. You did, you did, you promised!

KING. Doh . . .

BEAUTY. Thank you, dear father. You see – you do love me after all . . . Goodnight!

She exits.

KING. Goodnight. What have I done! What on earth am I going to do, there's not a yard of new cloth in the kingdom, and no spinning wheels to make any. Fool, fool, fool!

MINSTREL (*sung*).
    Fool, fool, fool.

KING. We can't, we mustn't.

MINSTREL (*sung*).
Such a foolish fool.

KING. But I promised her.

MINSTREL (*sung*).
Such a stupid, stupid fool.

KING *chases* MINSTREL *off.*

KING. Oh lordy. A new dress in one night . . . right. I'll make sure Beauty's locked up, I'll need an old carpenter.

GOODY *enters.*

You? What are you doing here? Oh no! Guards, guards!

GOODY. Wait, King! I've been here all the time, watching like you, to keep her from harm. It was a terrible thing I did.

KING. It was. Sixteen years of worry, not knowing when she might be taken from us . . .

GOODY. And I am truly sorry for it. But you are about to do worse, if you bring a spindle in here.

KING. But she wants a new dress for her birthday.

GOODY. Have it made somewhere else, and brought here.

KING. Her birthday's tomorrow.

GOODY. Give her something else.

KING. I promised her a dress, and I'll give her a dress! I only ever broke a promise once before, and look what happened! I'm not breaking this one. If you want to help me, and make up in some small way for your mistakes in the past, you'd be welcome. Otherwise, leave and never return. She must have a dress. Can you help?

GOODY. I could try.

KING. Then try. I'll keep her guarded. You have one night.

He exits.

GOODY. A dress. Quickly, Goody.

She spells.

Fair tides of good to you I kneel
Come prosper now this humble deal
And furnish I, that I might fly
Upon the fleetest spinning wheel.

She farts, a spindle magically appears, and GOODY *slowly starts to spin. As it speeds up, cloth starts to appear from everywhere.* GOODY *runs round collecting it as the spindle keeps turning.* BEAUTY *appears, astounded but unseen at first.*

It's working! It's working!

BEAUTY. Oh my! It's wondrous.

GOODY. What?

BEAUTY. It's so wondrous . . .

GOODY. Where are your guards?

BEAUTY. I saw it from my window and crawled out . . . oh, I wouldn't miss this for all the world! Who are you?

GOODY. I'm . . . I'm Goody.

BEAUTY. And what's this thing?

GOODY. Wait, stop, you musn't go near it.

BEAUTY. I only want to look.

GOODY. No!

They chase, BEAUTY *playful and* GOODY *desperate.* GOODY *tackles her to the floor. The cloth stops appearing, there is eerie sound, and the spindle stops turning.*

BEAUTY. What's happening?

GOODY. It's stopped . . . it's stopped. Perhaps you're safe . . .

The dress appears out of the cloth.

BEAUTY. What is that?

GOODY. It's your dress. It worked . . .

BEAUTY. My dress! You've made my dress! It's the most perfect in the world . . .

GOODY. Thank you.

BEAUTY. Can I put it on?

GOODY. No! It's . . . it's for tomorrow, you must go now.

BEAUTY. Please! I promise I won't tell, and I'll go straight after, I'll only try it on just to see if it fits, please Goody?

GOODY. Quickly then.

She dresses BEAUTY. BEAUTY *turns and turns.*

BEAUTY. It's beautiful!

GOODY. No. You're beautiful.

BEAUTY. I feel beautiful, for the first time in my life I feel beautiful.

A sound begins, which grows into an echo of the curse.

GOODY. Henbane and Monkshed, Nightshade and worse
Gather you here, and honour my curse.

The spindle starts turning again.

Oh no . . .

BEAUTY. Look, it's coming back.

GOODY. . . . please, no.

BEAUTY *walks toward the spindle, entranced, as the sound grows.*

She pricks her finger.

BEAUTY. Ouch.

She falls. The KING *and* QUEEN, COURTIERS *and* MINSTREL *come rushing in.*

I couldn't stop it . . .

QUEEN. Oh daughter . . .

A bell starts to ring midnight. KING *goes to* BEAUTY *and slowly picks up her sleeping body.*

KING. Sleep now, my only light. All will be dark for you now. Remember us when you wake, and know that you were loved, so loved . . . past midnight. Happy birthday Beauty.

The COURTIERS *sing a mournful Happy Birthday as he carries her to the bed. The* KING *lays her down on it.*

COURTIERS (*sung*).
　Blue sky, blue sky.

QUEEN. Beautiful as evening
　Graceful as the setting sun
　No voice now my angel
　And my grey skies they have just begun . . .

QUEEN. Oh my Beauty.

KING. My heart cannot bear this . . .

QUEEN. Hang on . . . the poison's on the needle, is that right?

GOODY. That's right.

QUEEN. Well if it worked for her . . . You!

COURTIER 3. Yes ma'am.

QUEEN. Give me your hand.

　She pricks a nearby COURTIER.

COURTIER. Ow.

　He falls asleep instantly.

KING. Good man!

QUEEN. Next!

COURTIER 1. What? But I've got a wife, and fourteen
　children.

　He is pricked, and falls asleep.

QUEEN. Next!

COURTIER 2. I'm allergic to needles, you can't . . . (*Pricked.*)

　He falls asleep. The MINSTREL *is hiding, but is
　discovered, and pricked.*

QUEEN. It's just us. Let us join our child, husband.

　She pricks KING.

KING. Ouch! (*Nothing happens.*) It's not working. (*Pricked
　again.*) Ouch! (*And again, and again.*) Ouch, ouch! I told
　you it's not working!

　He takes the needle and pricks her.

　See!

He pricks her again. She slaps him. They fight.

QUEEN. Husband!

KING. Wife!

They hug.

QUEEN. Cruel needle.

KING. Goody?

GOODY. It has run out. I cannot do a curse twice, King . . . sorry.

KING. We'll never see her awake again?

GOODY. No. She must wait for her prince, now.

KING. Oh dear. I hope he's a good man, whoever he is. And kind. I would've liked to have met him, by rights. How will he know she's here? Do you think we should . . . put up a sign?

GOODY. I'll try better.

She spells.

Come all the sprites and spirits here,
Come all ye wooded powers
Surround the sleeping princess
With a forest of rose-flowers.

She farts, and a forest of THORNS *springs up.*

What you? My magic.

The THORNS *laugh.*

KING. What's happened now? Call you these roses? Call you this magic? He'll never get to her now! You're not a fairy. You're a witch.

THORNS. Witch, witch.

QUEEN. You nasty, nasty weeds! Get away from my daughter!

GOODY. No Queen you mustn't.

QUEEN. I'll give you a pruning you'll never forget.

THORNS. Give you a pruning, give you a pruning.

But too late. She launches at the THORNS, *and they attack her, laughing as she is consumed or covered by them.*

KING. What? Darling? Where have you gone? Darling? Wife?

KING *launches into the thornbush, who give him very short shrift. He is about to be swallowed too . . .*

Fairy Goody! Be here. Wait for the prince. Make sure he knows . . .

He is consumed.

THORNS. Make sure he knows, make sure he knows.

The THORNS *fade away, and* GOODY *throws story dust. The* PRINCE OF QUESTIONS *is terrified by the deaths.*

GOODY. I tried to warn them . . . So that's how it's all come to this. Since, I've been here year upon year, lost count now, with nothing but waiting on a prince to wake her. And now you've come . . . prince?

He runs away.

Prince? Stop! Where are you going? Please, no! Stop! Run away . . . Oh no. But where is he? Where is the man strong enough to release her, and me . . . oh no.

She is interrupted by the entrance of an OGRESS, *dressed as a human. She is heavily pregnant and in the early stages of labour.*

Morning.

OGRESS. Yes it is.

GOODY. Who are you?

OGRESS. I am a queen. I'm looking for a fairy. I have heard there are fairies in this vicinity.

GOODY. Gone, long time since. Sorry, I.

OGRESS. I could smell you two miles away. Do not trifle with me. I need help.

GOODY. Yes?

OGRESS. I am . . . an Ogress.

GOODY. You don't look an ogress.

OGRESS. I've been on a diet.

GOODY. Meant I your clothing, and . . .

OGRESS. What?

GOODY. You look like a human.

OGRESS. Oh, I see. I married a human man.

GOODY. How strange.

OGRESS. I was forced to. I was forced to change. I forced myself to change.

GOODY. That can't have been easy.

OGRESS. No, and I fear it is about to get harder. You see, I'm pregnant.

GOODY. Congratulations.

OGRESS. You don't understand. It will be a human child. Ogres eat humans.

GOODY. Naturally.

OGRESS. Yes. But I do not want to eat my baby. I am desperate. Will you help me?

GOODY. I can't.

OGRESS. Why not?

GOODY. Because I must do good, and you're an ogress.

OGRESS. You would be saving my child's life, is that not good enough?

GOODY. Can't your kinghusband help you? Surely he understands.

OGRESS. My husband is dead.

GOODY. Dead . . .   .

OGRESS. I ate him. Unfortunately. (*She has a contraction.*) So you see my concern is pressing.

GOODY. Yes.

OGRESS. Yes.

GOODY. No.

OGRESS. What?

GOODY. I can't. For to help I'd need to go with you. And I made a solemn promise to meet a prince here and I have to stay.

OGRESS. When do you expect him?

GOODY. Soon. Ish. Sorry, I.

OGRESS. So am I. (*Contraction.*) Well, time moves on. Goodbye.

GOODY. Goodbye. And good luck with your son.

OGRESS. My son?

GOODY. Your baby. He's a boy.

OGRESS. A boy . . . A little prince . . . thank you.

She goes.

GOODY. Poor lady. No husband, and her an ogress in a human world. Strange child he'll turn out to be, if he escape her appetite – half ogre half human and ugly as a toad, I expect. Strong though. The strong prince . . . a strong prince! Wait. . . Queen! Queen! Wait!

She exits.

The Castle.

The OGRESS travels, pursued by GOODY, and the SLAVE appears as the OGRESS arrives at her castle.

The stage darkens. OGRESS crosses and has a final contraction.

OGRESS. Help me! Somebody help me . . .

She exits as GOODY arrives at the castle. It is grim and heavy.

There is a roaring offstage, hardly human.

GOODY. Sounds like it's going all natural.

The final roar ends. A smack and a child's cry is heard, and the OGRESS comes in with the baby PRINCE, besotted but petrified.

OGRESS. You came.

GOODY. Yes.

OGRESS. Thank you. Take him, quickly.

She hands GOODY *the baby.*

GOODY. He's beautiful.

OGRESS. I want to eat him . . .

The SLAVE *start chanting Carnem, Carnem during the scene.*

GOODY. Your highness, think what you do!

OGRESS. Help me, do something, do a spell.

GOODY. I can't.

OGRESS. You're a fairy, what do you mean you can't ooh soothe me.

GOODY. Soothe her, Goody, think.

OGRESS. I smell him.

GOODY. Think of something else! Think flowers, and, and butterflies.

OGRESS. No.

GOODY. Think rivers, and mountains.

OGRESS. No.

GOODY. Think stones.

OGRESS. No.

GOODY. I don't know how to soothe you, Queenie.

OGRESS. Then I must eat!

GOODY. Think Meat!

OGRESS. Urgh?

GOODY. Meat! Think meat! Think blood and bone, skin and muscle and meat!

OGRESS. Meat, yes!

The SLAVES *join in the naming of parts, and start chanting them.*

GOODY. Think eyes, think ears.

OGRESS. Yes . . .

GOODY. Think heart and lungs, gristle and fat and meat.

OGRESS. Oh . . .

GOODY. Think hair and nails, liver and spleen, think leg and arm and neck and belly and meat.

OGRESS. Oh yes . . .

GOODY. Think nose and tongue, finger and toe, think brains and kidney, guts and offal and meat.

OGRESS. Meat . . .

GOODY. Meat . . .

OGRESS. Meat . . .

GOODY. Meat.

The SLAVES' *chanting fades out. The* OGRESS *is satiated.* GOODY *slowly brings the baby to her. She holds him close.*

OGRESS. I feel strange.

GOODY. It's called love, Queenie.

She gently carries him out.

Now all I must do is be patient a while longer and keep her from eating the thing she loves most and into a strong handsome Prince he'll grow.

She exits. A time has passed. PRINCE *enters dashingly.*

PRINCE. Slaves! To the hunt!

The SLAVES *sing for him while he dances.*

SLAVES (*sung*).
   There was a young prince a handsome fellow
   dressed in red and gold
   astride his horse and lance in hand
   he ventured out so bold
   there never a fear came to his mind
   where'er he chose to ride
   with a heart as strong as sharp and bright
   as the sword worn at his side
   oh yes yes; yes, oh yes.

He scaled the craggy mountains and
he crossed the rivers wide
and from the gravest danger
never did he hide
he strode the forest at one step
the valleys he did tame
and all the goodly peasants did marvel at his fame
oh yes yes; yes, oh yes.

He took the stag fair by the horns
and wrestled to the floor
and when the beast was all tied up
he gave it to the poor
then the mighty grizzly bear he felled with just one hand
he surely is the bravest prince that ever walked the land
oh yes yes; yes oh yes oh yes.

OGRESS. Put him down! Slaves, get back to your cages. What are you doing today?

PRINCE. Just going to the woods.

OGRESS. Hunting again? Can't you give them a day off? Give them time to breed.

PRINCE. What does that mean?

OGRESS. Never mind. What are you hunting this time, my boy?

PRINCE. Don't know. Smelt some bears yesterday.

OGRESS. Come here. Don't be late. And don't talk to any strange women. And put some more clothes on, you'll get cold.

PRINCE. Yes Mother. See you later.

OGRESS. Ahem.

He goes to her, and kisses her on the cheek. OGRESS *exits.*

We are in the forest. GOODY *enters.*

PRINCE. Boo.

GOODY. Eek!

PRINCE. Got you.

GOODY. Swinepig. My breath's out with running, now my skin's off with fright, horrible boy.

PRINCE. Serves you right for scaring off the quarry. I nearly had a pair of wolves back there.

GOODY. Who eats wolves?

PRINCE. I'd have let them go again. So why were you after me? I'd have given you a lift if you'd said.

GOODY. I didn't want your mother knowing the reason, so.

PRINCE. Ooh, secrets.

GOODY. Now listen carefully, because this is very important. Once upon a time . . .

PRINCE. Snore.

GOODY. . . . long before you were born . . .

PRINCE. Snore.

GOODY. . . . when I was very young – why are you snoring?

PRINCE. Because you're boring.

GOODY. Fair said. Very near here there's a forest of terrible thorns.

PRINCE. Where?

GOODY. That way.

PRINCE. Want me to chop it down for you? No problem.

GOODY. No, or yes, but not for me. Behind that there's a beautiful palace.

PRINCE. Where? I've never seen it.

GOODY. It's hidden by the thorns.

PRINCE. Not for long Auntie.

GOODY. And that palace is peopled, full of sleeping people waiting to be woken.

PRINCE. Nice adventure. Let's do it.

GOODY. And the only one to wake them is a brave strong prince –

PRINCE. How convenient.

GOODY. – needs to find out the sleeping princess.

PRINCE. Easy.

GOODY. Go then to her chamber –

PRINCE. Time for some thorn-shearing.

GOODY. – and wake her –

PRINCE. Let's go.

GOODY. – with a kiss.

PRINCE. What?

GOODY. Here we are.

The THORNS *appear suddenly.*

THORNS. Here we are, hahaha.

PRINCE. Yes yes, very impressive, now shut up.

They quieten.

What did you say?

GOODY. You have to find the princess.

THORNS. Find the princess, find the princess.

PRINCE. No, after that.

THORNS. After that, after that.

GOODY. Kiss her, you have to kiss her.

THORNS. Kiss her, kiss her.

PRINCE. Uurgh . . .

GOODY. Eh?

PRINCE. Kiss? A Girl? Uurgh.

THORNS. Uurgh, uurgh.

GOODY. You need to wake her.

PRINCE. No thank you.

GOODY. But she's beautiful, most beautiful girl ever.

PRINCE. No way.

GOODY. Come, brave princey.

PRINCE. Uurgh.

THORNS. Uurgh, uurgh, hahaha.

GOODY. But the palace . . .

PRINCE. I don't care.

GOODY. Don't, please don't, please my only hope.

PRINCE. No. Absolutely no chance. I'm off, to find. . I don't
   know, something to kill.

THORNS. Something to kill, something to kill hahaha.

PRINCE. A girl? That is really disgusting. I'm going. Bye.

   He starts to exit.

GOODY. Coward.

THORNS. Coward.

PRINCE. Who said that?

   GOODY *goes behind* THORNS.

GOODY. Chicken.

THORNS. Chicken, chicken.

PRINCE. I'll give you chicken, you bunch of pansies.

GOODY. Buukbukbukbukbuk.

THORNS. Buukbukbukbukbukbukbukaak.

   He fights the THORNS. *They get the better of him, but after
   a struggle he breaks free.*

PRINCE. Not bad for a bunch of salad.

THORNS. Salad, hahaha.

PRINCE. Very fresh.

THORNS. Fresh, fresh.

PRINCE. Fresh and very captivating.

GOODY. Eh? You're supposed to fight them.

THORNS. Captivating, captivating.

PRINCE. Well you're very fresh, and you're extremely captivating. But I'm afraid you look like a bramble –

THORNS1-3. Bramble, hahaha!

PRINCE. – and your roots smell like shrivelled cabbage.

THORNS 2, 3. Cabbage, hahaha.

Thorn 1 scratches Thorn 2; they start fighting each other and it develops 'til they have gone off fighting.

PRINCE. Should keep them busy for a while. Plants are so stupid.

GOODY. You wondrous boy . . .

Eerie music starts (blue sky), and the bed is revealed, with BEAUTY *still asleep.*

PRINCE. What's going on?

GOODY. You've done it! You've unlocked the palace!

PRINCE. Have I? What's that noise?

GOODY. The whole palace, it's still here, just sleeping.

PRINCE. Wow. Weird.

GOODY. And here she is . . .

PRINCE. Who? Ow!

GOODY. The Princess Beauty.

PRINCE. Oh right.

GOODY. Well? Come see her.

PRINCE. No thanks. You know . . . don't want to disturb anyone.

GOODY. They want to be disturbed, so! That the whole purpose of –

PRINCE. It wasn't my purpose, my purpose was to go hunting you tricked me into coming here to fight your roses, wake your palace and don't think I don't know what you're after now. I'm not kissing her, or you, or anyone, so.

GOODY. Why not?

Pause.

PRINCE. I don't like girls, much.

GOODY. Have you ever met a girl?

PRINCE. Mother.

GOODY. A girl.

PRINCE. Well, you know, no. Mother won't let me.

GOODY. Thought I as much. Well, one's there, and very nice too.

PRINCE. No, I'll be fine.

GOODY. She won't bite you.

PRINCE. I'm fine. Well I'm not going to kiss her.

GOODY. Course you're not.

PRINCE. Wow . . .

GOODY. Beautiful, isn't she?

He leans over her, hesitates, and doesn't know what to do.

PRINCE. Here?

GOODY. Bit further up.

He smells her, licks her, is tempted to bite. His ogre-half is ruling.

PRINCE. Humaan . . .

GOODY. No!

He overcomes it, and is drawn to BEAUTY. *They kiss and* BEAUTY *wakes.*

PRINCE. I'm terribly sorry, I . . . I just . . .

The COURTIERS *and* MINSTREL *wake up. They see the* PRINCE *and* BEAUTY.

COURTIERS. Oooh . . .

MINSTREL (*sung*).
If you're ever faced with the forces of temptation . . .

COURTIERS. Just Say Yes
Just Say Yes, Yes, Yes.

BEAUTY *kisses the* PRINCE.

GOODY. It's done at last, and free I am! Oh wings, my wings of Goody, soon you'll be strong, and my magic shall return. I just need to see him home safe with his beautiful wife and I'll be a full fairy once again.

She leaves.

PRINCE. Um . . .

BEAUTY. What is it?

PRINCE. I'm afraid I've got to go.

BEAUTY. Go? Go where?

PRINCE. I'll come back. It's just . . . my mother will be worried.

BEAUTY. Oh . . . well I'll come with you.

PRINCE. No! I mean, not yet. I'll not be long, um . . .

BEAUTY. Beauty.

PRINCE. Beauty.

BEAUTY. Look, you're very nice and I'm sure your mother is too, but have you any idea how long I've been waiting?

She kisses him again, stopping him from going anywhere.

Elsewhere, the OGRE *finally frees himself from* GOODY*'s den.*

OGRE. FAIREE! FAIREE!

Sudden Blackout.

End of Act One.

ACT TWO

Song – Onceuponatime.

OGRE (*off*). FAIREE . . . FAIREE!

In the castle PRINCE, BEAUTY, OGRESS *and* GOODY *face each other.* PRINCE *and* BEAUTY *each hold a baby.*

PRINCE. Mother, this is Beauty. Beauty, this is my mother.

BEAUTY. And this is Rose, and this is Hector. Children, this is your grandmother.

OGRESS. You have been a long time hunting, my son.

PRINCE. Yes mother. Sorry mother.

OGRESS. Shall we eat?

GOODY *leaves to get the food. The* SLAVES *come on with chairs, led by the blind tableslave who is attached to the table.*

SLAVES (*sung*).
Oh ye, oh ye
Oh ye who pass this way
Come caring, come daring
Take comfort while ye may.

Oh ye, oh ye
Oh ye who venture in
Come doubting come shouting
Ye are all men of sin.

Oh ye, oh ye
Oh ye who walk this hall
Come starving come carving
The worm shall eat you all.

The SLAVE *and table are set.*

BEAUTY. . . . so the curse stated that only a brave prince could wake me, and fortunately, your son discovered me and well, here we are! Grandmother?

OGRESS. Uurgh . . . pardon?

BEAUTY. Did Goody not tell you all of this?

OGRESS. She did not. And how did you come to discover the sleeping princess, son?

PRINCE. Well Goody told me all about her and led me to the thorns and . . . that if . . . um . . .

GOODY. Ahem.

Pause. The OGRESS *glares at* GOODY, *who has come up with the food.*

OGRESS. Did she indeed. Well.

GOODY. Dinner is served.

Food is served. BEAUTY, PRINCE *and the* OGRESS *sit down,* PRINCE *and* BEAUTY *opposite each other,* OGRESS *opposite the children, at whom she stares.*

BEAUTY. What is this meat, grandmother?

OGRESS. Baby . . .

OGRESS. Baby pig. Baby pig provencale.

BEAUTY. Oh . . .

It is interrupted by a roar from the OGRE.

OGRE (*off*). FAIREE . . .

Everyone freezes. Only the OGRESS *and* GOODY *recognise the sound.*

GOODY. Oh no . . .

BEAUTY. What was that noise, darling?

PRINCE. Nothing to worry about, I'll sort it out.

OGRESS. Wait. You haven't eaten.

PRINCE. But mother . . .

OGRESS. Ignore it, and it will go away. Goody?

GOODY. Yes, Queenie?

OGRESS. More meat.

OGRE. FAIREE . . .

SLAVES. Ahh!

BEAUTY. What is it?

OGRESS. It's nothing. Carry on.

BEAUTY. It doesn't sound like nothing.

OGRE. WHERE ARE YOU, FAIREE?

SLAVES. Aah!

PRINCE. Right.

OGRESS. Do as you're told, and stay there.

BEAUTY *goes to the children. During the scene she picks up Hector.*

BEAUTY. Don't you worry my darlings I'm here, your father's here.

PRINCE. Mother.

OGRESS. What?

PRINCE. I'm not hungry. Can I get down now please?

OGRESS. No you can't.

BEAUTY. Why do you want to get down, darling?

OGRESS. You haven't eaten.

OGRE. I'VE COME FOR YOU.

SLAVES. Aah!

BEAUTY. How dreadful.

PRINCE. It's nothing to worry about, darling.

OGRE. I CAN SMELL YOU . . .

SLAVES. Aah! Aah! It can smell us, it can smell us!

All the SLAVES *are now panicking.*

OGRESS. Silence!

PRINCE. Right. I'm going to kill it.

BEAUTY. You're not going out there?

OGRESS. Sit down!

OGRE. I KNOW YOU'RE IN THERE.

SLAVE 1. There it is! There it is! There it is! It's huge and terrifying and covered in hair and chains and blood and oh my life my short and meaningless life . . . (*etc.*)

BEAUTY. WHAT IS IT?

OGRESS. It's an ogre.

The servants go into mayhem, a cacophony of fear and blind panic, during which Rose is hidden under the OGRESS' *dress.*

PRINCE. Silence! Silence you bunch of gutless yellow-bellied feathered invertebrates! Just get a grip on your quivering excuses for selves, get me my horse, and leave this uncivilised peabrain to me.

BEAUTY. Don't leave us!

OGRESS. No, my son, I cannot allow.

PRINCE. Mother, on this occasion.

OGRESS. I am the queen, and I say you shall not go, it's far too dangerous.

PRINCE. Well I am the Prince, and I say I shall.

OGRE. THEN I'M COMING IN.

SLAVES. AHH! AHH!

OGRESS. Shut up! You do not know what this means, my son.

PRINCE. I've never had the chance to fight an ogre.

OGRESS. We've got an army for things like this.

PRINCE. That bunch of wimps? They're probably hiding.

SLAVES. Hide! Hide!

The SLAVES *run away, except the* TABLE-SLAVE, *who cannot.*

PRINCE. You think I'm a child Mother, but I'm not. I've got a wife and two children, and I love them more than anything in the world . . . can I get down?

OGRESS. Yes.

BEAUTY. But can't you protect us from here? I want you to stay, husband, and I am the Princess, and your wife . . .

OGRESS. His mind is made up. He must go.

PRINCE. I'll be back soon. Please don't worry. Stay here. You'll be safest indoors.

He exits.

BEAUTY. Safest indoors . . . that's what my Father said.

TABLE-SLAVE (*sung*).
There was a young prince, a handsome fellow
Dressed in gold and red
He ventured out to fight the beast
And ended up quite d . . .

OGRESS *shuts him up.*

BEAUTY. My poor dear, it's all been very scary, hasn't it? Shh now, shhh, be strong, strong like your sister . . . Rose? Rose? Where's Rose?

OGRESS. I don't know. Perhaps she got lost in the melee.

BEAUTY. Got lost? But she can't even walk.

OGRESS. Perhaps she crawled.

BEAUTY. I'll go and look, she can't have got far . . . Rose? Rose?

She takes Hector and leaves. OGRESS *takes Rose out from under her skirt, and puts her on the table in front of her.*

OGRESS. So, little child. Your father loves you more than anything in the world . . .

SLAVES *start chanting Carnem, as* BEAUTY *and the* OGRE *search.*

OGRE. Fairee. . .

BEAUTY. Rose? Rose?

GOODY *rushes in.*

OGRESS. Goody.

GOODY. Sorry, Queenie, I was just . . . making dessert.

OGRESS. Too early.

GOODY. What? But you said.

OGRESS. I will have one more dish of meat.

GOODY sees Rose.

GOODY. No, no, no no no no, think about blood and bone and skin and muscle.

OGRESS. SILENCE! Take her.

GOODY. Yes take her, I'll take her.

GOODY takes Rose.

OGRESS. To the kitchen.

GOODY. Highness, no . . .

OGRESS. Grill her.

GOODY. No! Think brain and toe and . . .

OGRESS. You betrayed me by bringing my son to the Princess, by bringing an ogre to my door, and by bringing temptation to my table. You have failed me Goody and now you must pay. Grill her or I will eat you, then her, raw and alive. Knife!

A butcher's knife appears, handed to GOODY. OGRESS *exits, leaving* GOODY *with the baby and only the tableslave for company.*

GOODY. For the wings of angels, I cannot cook no babies . . . what has happened you, Queenie?

OGRESS (*from off*). More Meat!

GOODY. Oh, nature help me now . . . My magic! Perhaps it has returned
I must try, I must try . . .

She spells.

Coven court of shady deeding
Help me now the ogress feeding
Grilled and shaped to my own needing
With stumps and edges still a-bleeding.

Nothing happens.

Nothing.

She lets out a long, weak fart.

TABLE-SLAVE. Heeheehee.

GOODY. What?

TABLE-SLAVE (*blows imitation raspberry*). Heeheehee   .

GOODY. Thinks it funny, do you?

TABLE-SLAVE. Eat you raw, she will heeheehee.

GOODY. My magic gone, the babe to be killed, and you laugh.

TABLE-SLAVE. Poor little fartbum heehee.

GOODY. Laugh again and it's you she'll be eating instead of
the baby.

Pause. GOODY *does another small fart.*

TABLE-SLAVE. Heehee.

GOODY. Good man.

GOODY *advances, knife drawn, and prepares to chop his
arm off.*

TABLE-SLAVE. What? No! You cheated! I'm sorry! No,
please! How can it be better to kill me than the baby? I'm
still human! And she'll know, I'm all ragged and boney
she'll know, please, no . . .

GOODY. Well then I needs find something else to feed her.
Any ideas?

TABLE-SLAVE. There's Lavinia.

GOODY. Lavinia?

TABLE-SLAVE. My new donkey, in the stable.

GOODY. Thank you.

GOODY *rushes off, chases the* DONKEY *on and then off to
the kitchens.*

TABLE-SLAVE. That was a present from my old mum . . .

The TABLE-SLAVE *weeps, as the* DONKEY *is cooked,*
BEAUTY *searches for Rose, the* OGRE *searches for*
GOODY *and the* PRINCE *searches for the* OGRE.

OGRE. Fairee!

OGRESS enters, as GOODY enters with the meal. OGRESS eats, as the TABLE-SLAVE suffers. GOODY exits as BEAUTY enters with the sleeping Hector.

BEAUTY. Rose? Rose?

OGRESS. Still no sign?

BEAUTY. Where could she have got to? Oh dear . . .

OGRESS. Is there anything I can do?

BEAUTY. Could you hold Hector? I'll have a better look. Your castle is so dark, he's terrified, the poor sweet thing.

OGRESS. Sweet thing . . .

OGRESS takes Hector. BEAUTY exits calling for Rose. OGRESS takes Hector's hat off, smells it, and puts it on the table.

Goody!

GOODY. Highness?

OGRESS. More meat. In a cream sauce.

GOODY. Please no.

OGRESS. Do not fail me.

She hands Hector to GOODY, and exits.

The chanting continues as GOODY turns to TABLE-SLAVE.

GOODY. Any ideas?

TABLE-SLAVE. Nothing.

GOODY. I saw a cat in your garden.

TABLE-SLAVE. No! No! Please not Lucky! Leslie, my goat, by the midden-heap.

GOODY. Thank you.

GOODY dashes off, chases on GOAT, exits with it and Hector. BEAUTY enters as OGRESS enters.

BEAUTY. Rose? I can't find her. Is Hector coping?

OGRESS. He's done very well, the saucey boy.

BEAUTY. Where is he? I can't see him anywhere.

GOODY *enters with food, which* OGRESS *starts to eat.*
Hector's hat is still on the table.

BEAUTY. Why there's his hat. Where is he? What have you
done with him? Hector . . .   .

OGRESS. Sweet, as you said.

BEAUTY. My son . . .

OGRESS. Now you know. So now you must also be cooked.

GOODY. It is a wicked thing, Queenie.

OGRESS. Do you think I have any choice? I am what I am!

GOODY. There is no good in this.

OGRESS. I have hidden it for too long. Kill her, cook her, and
then leave. Your work is done. And Fairy . . . I will just eat
her heart.

She exits. BEAUTY *screams.*

GOODY. Princess, oh princess.

BEAUTY. My babies, my sweet babies . . .

GOODY. Shh, princess, and listen.

BEAUTY. No! You heard what she said. Go on. Kill me. Kill
me too and take me to my darlings, you treacherous,
scheming murderer. My babies . . .

GOODY. Listen to I, princess.

BEAUTY. I was truly cursed the day I was born.

GOODY. No, hark now.

BEAUTY. Do what you must, I do not care. My babies . . .

GOODY. Your babies are well.

BEAUTY. What?

GOODY. Shh! Your babies are well and alive, and hid away.
Think I a murderer?

BEAUTY. Alive? Where are they? Let me see them!

GOODY. Later.

BEAUTY. NOW.

> GOODY *gets the children.*

My darlings . . . I'm sorry. Never again will I leave you.

OGRESS (*off*). More meat!

BEAUTY. Tell me, why is this happening.

GOODY. Queenie is . . .

BEAUTY. Is what?

GOODY. . . . an Ogress.

BEAUTY. An ogress . . .

GOODY. She wanted to eat them, but I switched them with . . . something else and so on and she is fooled, so.

BEAUTY. An Ogress? But how is she queen and . . . she is the Prince's mother?

GOODY. Oh yes.

BEAUTY. Then he must be an . . . oh no . . .

OGRESS (*from off*). Meat, Goody.

BEAUTY. Oh no.

GOODY. What to do with Queenie now . . .

BEAUTY. Can't you poison her?

GOODY. Supposed to be a fairy, I, and do good . . .

BEAUTY. But you would be doing good by killing her.

GOODY. If a fairy kills, the fairy dies, and I don't want to die.

BEAUTY. We will all die! You must do it!

GOODY. But it's natural so, for an Ogress, she suffers from the strongest urges.

BEAUTY. Well so do I, and if you don't do something then I'll go in and kill her myself.

GOODY. You will fail.

BEAUTY. Then you do something. Why not make her sleep for a few years – you're good enough at that I seem to remember.

OGRESS (*off*). MORE MEAT!

BEAUTY. Children, hold tight, we're going for a little walk.

GOODY. Where?

BEAUTY. Anywhere but here. To the Forest.

GOODY. You mustn't, gentle princess, it is full of danger.

BEAUTY. There is no safe place for me, not now. I'll try and find my husband and if you care for light, and life, and goodness, you will find the courage to finish her.

She exits with the children.

GOODY. I care about my wings! I care about 100 years of waiting! If I give her a death spell, I'll never spell again! But wait, wait . . . food! What will I do for meat now . . .

OGRESS enters.

OGRESS. I'm waiting . . .

GOODY goes off. OGRESS sits at table, next to desperate TABLE-SLAVE. A cat's miaow can be heard, before being strangled.

TABLE-SLAVE. Oh no . . .

Carnem continues to be sung by the SLAVE.

From off there is the sound of chopping, cooking etc. GOODY re-enters with food, gives it to OGRESS. She eats.

OGRESS. Now I am truly soothed. You may go.

GOODY leaves.

OGRESS begins to choke. She coughs up a small collarbell. She rings it.

TABLE-SLAVE. Lucky! Lucky, you're still alive!

OGRESS. What . . .

TABLE-SLAVE. My faithful cat, Lucky! I thought she'd cooked it, that terrible, murderous cook but no, she's alive, she's ali . . .

OGRESS. A cat? I have eaten a cat?

OGRESS is sick all over the TABLE-SLAVE, and everywhere.

Run, little fairy. RUN! I am after you! I am after you all!

She exits, leaving a distraught TABLE-SLAVE.

TABLE-SLAVE. Gone, all gone . . . what more can happen to me now?

The OGRE *finally breaks in, furious. The other* SLAVES *disappear.*

OGRE. Where is the fairee?

TABLE-SLAVE. Oh yes, join in why don't you.

OGRE. Humaan!

He goes up to TABLE-SLAVE *and goes to bite; stops.*

Uurgh . . .

TABLE-SLAVE. What?

OGRE. Why are you covered in bits of cat?

TABLE-SLAVE. Oh Lucky . . .

OGRE. Where is it?

TABLE-SLAVE. What?

OGRE. THE FAIREE.

TABLE-SLAVE. Gone, gone.

OGRE. Where?

TABLE-SLAVE. Off to murder someone else's friends I shouldn't wonder.

OGRE. I do not like her, she tricked me.

TABLE-SLAVE. You should hear what she done to me, mate.

OGRE. Why are you wearing a table?

TABLE-SLAVE. It's not a table, it's a necklace.

OGRE *doesn't get it.*

I'm a slave, you wazzock! D'you think I've got a choice, think I'm wearing it for the good of me health, what it's a fashion item is it? Great hairy . . .

OGRE *goes to him.*

Oh now you're going to kill me, I suppose. Go on then, do your worst what are you doing? Hey!

The OGRE *takes the table off him.*

No what are you doing? Argh! You've taken off my . . . you've taken off my table! Oh thank you! I'm free! I'm free! I want to hug you! Where are you, you lovely great thing you, come here!

He runs blindly off, and has an accident.

OGRE. Humans are so stupid. FAIREE!

He exits.

The Forest.

BEAUTY *runs on with the children, looks round, and runs off again.*

The PRINCE *enters, hunting the ogre.*

PRINCE. Where are you, you Dodo?

OGRE (*off*). FAIREE.

PRINCE. Time for some extinction.

PRINCE *follows the sound off.*

GOODY *enters out of breath.*

GOODY. Prince? Beauty? Where are you?

The OGRESS *enters.*

Queenie! Finished your meal already?

OGRESS. You betrayed me again.

GOODY. Yes. It was for the good, Queenie.

OGRESS. For whose good? Fairies taste very bitter, I'm told.

GOODY. Yes.

OGRESS. I shall have to spit you out.

GOODY *runs off,* OGRESS *in pursuit.*

BEAUTY *runs on, carrying the children.*

BEAUTY. Husband? Husband where are you? Where are you?

The THORNS *appear round her.*

THORNS. Beauty! Beauty!

The OGRESS *enters.*

BEAUTY. Help, protect me!

THORNS. Protect me, protect me!

The THORNS *attack the* OGRESS *but she grasps*
BEAUTY*'s dress.*

BEAUTY *takes off the dress, and escapes with the children.*

OGRESS *exits after them.*

The OGRE *enters, finds the dress, and smells it.*

OGRE. Humaan . . .

PRINCE (*off*). I can smell you, you great slug.

GOODY (*off*). Prince! Prince!

The OGRE *hears something, goes to a den and climbs in.*
There is a creature in there whom he evicts or kills. He
hides.

PRINCE *runs on after the* OGRE, *but stops at the dress.*

PRINCE. Now I'm onto you, wartface! Beauty's dress?
Beauty? Where are you, Beauty? Where are my children?

OGRE (*off*). Humaan.

PRINCE. The ogre . . .

OGRESS (*off*). Humaan.

PRINCE. Two ogres! Oh my darlings, my poor helpless
darlings.

GOODY *enters.*

GOODY. Prince? Prince!

PRINCE. My darlings . . .

GOODY. Hurry now, you must come back.

PRINCE. The Ogre has eaten Beauty.

GOODY. No no, I tricked her.

PRINCE. Her dress.

GOODY. No listen, she was after eating them but she didn't,
    you must come back.

Next two speeches are spoken simultaneously:

PRINCE. No, The Ogre's eaten Beauty! Look her dress,
    I found it here and no sign of them, no I was tracking the
    Ogre and was nearly on him when no where are my
    children, where's my wife . . . what?

GOODY. Listen now you must come back, there's no time
    now, your mother's gone all natural, listen to me she wanted
    to eat the children, thinks she has, and Beauty listen, but
    I tricked her and now Beauty's left and into the forest and
    your mother is gone blood-crazy.

PRINCE. Who's gone blood-crazy?

GOODY. I'm trying to tell you.

PRINCE. What's happened? Where's Beauty? Where are my
    children? Who's gone blood-crazy?

GOODY. I'm trying to tell you . . . your mother . . .

PRINCE. What? My mother what?

GOODY. Your mother . . . is an . . .

The OGRE *appears from the den.*

OGRE. FAIREE!

*GOODY yelps and runs off, OGRE goes to pursue but is
stopped by the PRINCE, sword in hand.*

PRINCE. Now you're what I call ugly.

He swings for the OGRE, who catches his hand easily.

OGRE. You what I call breakfaast.

*The OGRE is about to bite him when he catches a whiff of
him.*

Humaan . . . huh? Ogaar! Baby Ogaar!

PRINCE. What?

OGRE. You an ogaar! (*Smells again.*) No, humaan . . . ogaar. .
    I am confused. . .

PRINCE *breaks free*.

PRINCE. No, just a bit prehistoric.

PRINCE *swings for him again, but* OGRE *catches him again.*

OGRE. Don't make me kill you!

PRINCE. Sorry.

OGRE (*smells again*). Ogaar . . . no, humaan . . . what are you? WHAT ARE YOU?

PRINCE. Mother . . . Mother!

OGRE. Mother? Yes . . . where is your mother?

PRINCE. I don't know.

OGRE. We will find your mother . . .

PRINCE. Mother!

The OGRE *drags him off.*

GOODY *comes back on.*

GOODY. Oh no . . . what have I done.

The THORNS *spring up.*

THORNS. What have I done, what have I done.

They grab her.

GOODY. What? You again?

THORNS. You again! You again!

She drives them back with a spell.

GOODY. Tooth of boar and sorrelsprig
For roses now deadheaded
Cleft your twines and leave your spines
All in the earth embedded.

She farts, and the THORNS *shrink back into the earth.*

And stay there! But . . . my magic! My magic is returning! Quickly, the Prince, no, Beauty, no. . anyone! I'm coming!

She exits.

BEAUTY *runs on with the kids, exhausted.*

BEAUTY. I can't go any further. We've run so far, she can't have followed us.

OGRESS (*appearing*). Oh but I have.

BEAUTY. You! Oh no . . .

OGRESS. I smelt you, you see. Humans are surprisingly ill-equipped for this harsh world. And now I must have the children.

BEAUTY. They are your own flesh, your own blood . . . how can you eat them? Have you no love for them?

OGRESS. I love my son, and he loves you, and I am . . . I am sorry, Princess, but I am so hungry.

BEAUTY. You will have to kill me first.

OGRESS. If you insist.

BEAUTY. Oh husband. Where is my brave prince now?

OGRESS moves towards BEAUTY, who is too tired to fight.

PRINCE. Mother! Mother!

The OGRE throws the PRINCE on, and enters.

BEAUTY. Husband.

OGRE walks on, slowly.

OGRE. What is he?

OGRESS. He is my son.

OGRE. He has Ogaar blood.

OGRESS. Yes.

OGRE. His father?

OGRESS. His mother.

She removes her head covering, and reveals herself as an ogre. The PRINCE shrinks from her.

My son . . .

The PRINCE moves away.

OGRE. You are . . .

OGRESS. Yes. I am an Ogress.   .

PRINCE. Mother . . .

OGRE. It is against our laws. It is unnatural. It must not be. It will not be.

He raises his club to strike the PRINCE, *and the* OGRESS *leaps forward.*

They fight, but the OGRE *is stronger. He kills the* OGRESS.

GOODY *rushes on.*

GOODY. Sorry I'm late.

The OGRE *lets the body of the* OGRESS *fall, looks at* GOODY.

OGRE. FAIREE!

GOODY. Quick, Goody, thinks.

He raises his club towards her.

There is nothing else . . . oh, my wings, my life.

She spells.

Oh coven of blackness mother of all
I chant the spell of my final breath
Fair circle of nature on him fall
Give him his death.

There is an almighty puff of smoke and sparks, and the OGRE *dies.*

Everyone falls back except GOODY. *She farts long and slow as she crumples.*

BEAUTY. Husband . . .

PRINCE. My Beauty.

They hug.

Mother . . . she's died. Trying to save me . . .

BEAUTY. And trying to kill us.

PRINCE. Where are the children?

BEAUTY. They are safe.

He goes to them – she moves away.

PRINCE. What?

BEAUTY. Stay away.

PRINCE. I don't understand.

BEAUTY. You are her son.

PRINCE. Beauty?

BEAUTY. The son of an Ogress.

PRINCE. But . . .

BEAUTY. No! Keep away from us.

PRINCE. But I love you . . . I love you Beauty, and Hector, and Rose.

BEAUTY. And I love you, but I'm frightened. I don't know what to do.

There is a groaning, and GOODY *comes round. Her wings have fallen off.*

PRINCE. Auntie.

GOODY. What? Still here? Where's the Ogre.

PRINCE. You killed him, Auntie . . .

BEAUTY. You saved us. Thank you . . . but I thought you said if a fairy kills –

GOODY. – the fairy dies . . . why aren't I dead then? My wings! My . . . they've fallen off. My last fairy breath, it must have meant. No longer a fairy . . . and just as my magic was coming again.

A pause, as the others take on this loss.

Queenie.

BEAUTY. She died, fighting the Ogre.

PRINCE. Protecting me.

BEAUTY. And trying to kill us.

PRINCE. Yes I know, I know.

BEAUTY. Please stay away.

GOODY. Eh?

PRINCE. She won't let me hold her, or the children Auntie, she thinks I'm going to eat my own family.

BEAUTY. Your own family has been chasing me round the forest half the night.

PRINCE. And your own family has been chasing round trying to protect you.

GOODY. Stop it, stop it! I've lost one hundred years trying to get you two together. I've lost my wings and I'm about to lose my temper. You've got love and life, and neither lasts for long, so please just get on with it.

PRINCE *goes to kiss* BEAUTY, *she pulls away.*

PRINCE. Have I ever tried to bite you?

BEAUTY. No.

PRINCE. If I ever do . . .

BEAUTY. I'll bite you back. Harder.

They kiss. As the lights fade:

FOREST CREATURES (*sung*).
Seed and acorn hoof and horn
all that dies must be reborn
from dusk til dawn til eve til morn
flesh shall grow, flesh shall grow, flesh shall grow . . .

The End.

THE MUSIC

1. Hoof and Horn

words by Rufus Norris
music by Richard Chew

2. Just Say No

words by Rufus Norris
music by Richard Chew

3. Blue Sky (*Mourning Song*)

words by Rufus Norris
music by Richard Chew

4. Men of Sin

words by Rufus Norris
music by Richard Chew

5. Huntsong

words by Rufus Norris
music by Richard Chew

There was a young prince, a hand-some fel-low dressed in red and gold ast-ride his horse with lance in hand he ven-tured out so bold There nev-er a fear came to his mind where-'er he chose to ride with a heart as strong and sharp and bright as the sword worn at his side Oh

yes, __ oh yes oh yes oh yes oh yes __ oh yes, oh yes. He

yes, __ oh yes oh yes oh yes oh yes __ oh yes, oh yes.

yes, __ oh yes oh yes oh yes oh yes __ oh yes, oh yes.

6. Carnem
meatsong

words by Rufus Norris
music by Richard Chew